# "I AM MORE!" ®

I AM MORE: The Journey

# I AM MORE!

## The Journey

### SIGNATURE EDITION

**TONISHA "DR. TONI" PINCKNEY**

I AM MORE: The Journey

TONISHA "DR. TONI" PINCKNEY

I AM MORE – the Journey
ISBN-13: 978-0692674321
ISBN-10: 0692674322
Copyright © 2009, 2016 by Tonisha Pinckney
Published by
I AM MORE Institute for Excellence and Social Responsibility, Inc.

Send Inquiries to I AM MORE Institute:
sales@iammoreonline.com
www.iammoreonline.com

# Table of Contents

# DEDICATION

**This book** is dedicated to every lady, gentleman, and child who was told they were nothing.

**This journey** is dedicated to every surviving victim of domestic violence, rape, incest, emotional abuse, suicide attempts, or any other event which was orchestrated to end your life rather than fulfill your dreams.

**My words** are dedicated to those who lost their footing following in the steps of others.

**My poems** are dedicated to those who know they are more, but forgot how to say it or just did not have the courage.

**The lessons** are dedicated to my children.

## ACKNOWLEDGEMENTS

Loretta Stevens, my mother, pastor of Community House of Prayer (Newark, NJ)

In memory of Elder John G. Stevens, Sr. (1952-2005)

DaVante' & Jordon Pinckney, Morrisa, Naomi & Johnnie Stevens, Sonia Martinez, James Pedersen, Ellis and Tina Still,

*Thank you all for love, support, and truth!*

## FORWARD

I have worked in the mental health field for approximately 9 years with 4 years on an assertive community treatment team. I am proud to work on a psychiatric multi-disciplinary team whose focus is keeping adults with mental illness out of the hospital and in the community focusing on person-centered goals. In 2008, I also started working with substance abuse clients who are now working on recovery based on an abstinence model.

As the mother of a globally developmentally delayed 11 year old son, I constantly struggle with having my son viewed as a strong and exceptional young man. Many see him as being limited by his disabilities. I advocate for people to recognize and focus on his abilities. While he does require some understanding, in most ways he is no different than any other boy his age. As I read this book, I realized I can show him he is more than a label! I can tell him and my clients that things from our past do not have the power to define who we are in our present.

This book gives people the courage and permission to move past their past looking toward a more positive future. A future is attainable when you're able to forgive. In my work with those fighting substance abuse, I can see they are stuck. They are trapped in a place of negative voices and images telling them what they were, who they are, and replaying the tragedies they have lived. This book will help them get back the self-esteem which was lost or even never had the opportunity to foster.

The easy to follow reading and guided journal give people the chance to reflect on how they can be more. They have the opportunity to own personal struggles and turn them into successes. I AM MORE gives the control back to the reader and gives points the reader toward a purposeful future loaded with prospects of mental, emotional, economic, and spiritual prosperity.

-Karetha Henry, CASAC, MSW

## INTRODUCTION

When discussing this book with my 10 year-old son, he asked if he was *more* too. I immediately said, "Of course, baby. We all are "more." The question triggered a whole line of thinking for me. Initially, the concept of this book was geared toward ladies ages 16-50. However, after I spoke at various places, listened to children, gleaned from the wisdom of those over 50, and heard the cry of men, I realized this book would be for everyone. Pain has no age, race, color, creed, religious, sexual, or gender preferences. We all experience pain. I experienced pain from childhood on. The source of some my pain resulted from a man hurting so bad internally that he only knew how to hurt; and boys who did not understand the lasting effects of pain and rage on the life of another person. Some of my pain was also due to a son who grew up constantly being told by his mother he was unwanted, causing him not to know how to love and respect his wife, the mother of his children, I can see how pain begat pain. It is my goal to end the cycle. I use my pain to identify pain.

I have included four poems which express different outlooks on being *more*. For the lady – "I AM MORE". For the child – "I Am a Child, But I Am More". For the spiritual person – "He is More, So I Am More". For the gentleman – Standing Strong, I AM MORE". One of the selections I hope you will enjoy reading is the award-winning poem written by my ten-year-old son entitled "Who Am I", which he had submitted to the town poetry contest.

Not really knowing how this series of poems affected him, I had to ask my son over and over again what he thought. He gave me the quick 10-year old expected answer – "It's cool mom. You're awesome." But, it was while reading his poem that I felt a new and unique pride. The poem was not a question he asked himself. It was an answer to the questions which were asked of him many times. Who are you? What do you want to do with your life? His answers were decisive, assertive and strong. They also contained doubt or slightly diminished self-esteem. I remember thinking - I wish I had known myself so well at age ten, twenty or twenty-nine. I could not answer those questions until I was thirty. Even then, I was still in the midst of the process.

This book itself is a process. It is a journey. It is a journey I completed over the span of my life. The path was one I did not know or understand. It is, therefore, a journey I still take again from time to time. There is no need to address all the questions parents, teachers, and society as a whole ask of us every day. As I take you on a journey from "I AM ME!" to "I AM MORE", you might realize who you are and how much more you can become.

I am not a therapist, counselor, or doctor. I am a lady who has endured too much, too young, and for too long. I am standing on the other side with my tired arms raised shouting "I AM MORE"! I am not wearing badges of independence, domestic violence, abuse, or any other label of victimization. I am simply holding my tired back straight, facing forward, and after a long, deep breath saying "I AM MORE!"

I AM MORE: The Journey

# *PART ONE:*

## THE UNDERSTANDING
### "I AM ME!"

## Who is Dr. Toni?

**I am me!**

A strong, single, black woman who loves her children.

**I am me!**

A lady who loves deeply. A person who tries hard to bring happiness to others.

**I am me!**

Like anyone else I've been hurt and I survived! I survived rape. I survived domestic violence. I survived abuse. I survived the system that was meant to protect me. I survived the doubt that was meant to destroy me. I survived the fight against myself.

**I am who I am - not who I was - and rapidly becoming who God predestined me to be.**

I am a mother, a friend, a sister, a daughter, a small

business owner, a forensic accountant, a student, an author, a poet, an intercessor, a believer, a Christian, a lover of mankind, an exerciser of faith, and ever evolving. I am emotional yet strong. I am distant yet compassionate. I know my calling, my purpose, and the power of my testimony.

**I am more than society says I am - I am me!**

**I am more than I ever thought I would be - I am me!**

## Who are you?

You are a culmination of morals, ethics, values, ideas, experiences, dreams, desires, and so on. Like a cake, you are made up of perfectly measured ingredients which come together to create your taste, appearance, and presentation. Your ingredients are your past, various roles, job/career, decisions, thoughts, vision, and destiny. You need to comfortably and proudly say "I AM ME!" before you can truly say "I AM MORE".

It is in knowing yourself that you acknowledge you have not reached your full potential. The space of knowing you is also a place of knowing your limitations. In order to expand your territory, you must expand your thinking. Before you can expand your thinking, you have to begin with knowing who you are and what you think of yourself. This is

I AM MORE: The Journey

also how you will be able to look at others and recognize when they do not see the valuable you – the real you – the you who is emerging.

Who are you? What are your talents, desires, or gifts? What role do you play in the lives of others? Your "I AM ME!" statement is not about feeling or emotion. It excludes how others perceive you or feel about you. For example, a cake can look delicious. However, some people will like it and some won't. Some may respond to the taste of the ingredients differently. Others, due to their own personal preferences, may decide not to taste the cake at all. This does not change what the cake is. It is the cakes job to be a cake – nothing more – nothing different.

You are the same way. Your task is to be you. Others will admire or even detest parts of you. But, you must be strong enough to know this does not change your "I AM ME!" statement. Your statement may evolve over time. It could begin with, "I am a daughter/son". Today you may say, "I am a single woman/man". Next, your statement may change to "I am a husband/wife". Then you might add mother/father, grandparent, etc. You may have evolved the statement from student to teacher. Even after you become a teacher, you will still be a student – always learning so you can teach. All of this does not change who you are as a person, but how you evolved into a new role. You will always be those things. If your role changes in life, you may have to edit your statement. However, you should keep your "I AM ME!" statements and look back at them from time to time. Ask yourself how your roles have changed. Have you added new relationships or are you in different positions?

Your role does not define you. The "I AM ME!" statement is not about defining yourself by your roles. Quite the contrary, it is meant to define your attitude about you and your roles. For instance – today is a good or bad day depending on how you perceive it. You are a mother, father, husband, wife, student, or teacher whether or not you are good or bad at it. When you own a role, then you can define it.

Disconnect the limitation. Stop saying, "I am not a good friend". Say, "I am a friend". "Not a good" is the limiting agent. The same is true if you say, "I am a good friend". "A good" is limiting. Both limit you from properly assessing yourself. You are a friend. At times, you may be a great friend. Other times you may be a horrible friend. The constant is friend. You are a friend. How will you know when to either improve or stop being hard on yourself if you permanently connect the adjective to the noun. In your "I AM ME!" statement you say "I am a friend". Adjectives like good and bad are subjective. The meanings can change depending on the day, the emotion, or the people involved.

When pondering the idea of being *more*, you are

encouraged to assess what type of friend you are to others. You can then decide whether you need to be a better friend to others or a better friend to yourself. Before you can assess an idea, you must first identify it.

My statement includes my spirituality. I feel the main focus in my life is God. So I have included aspects of that relationship in my statement. As I get closer to God and learn more about Him, I learn more about myself. I am intelligent. But, it is in prayer I learn that I am wise. My "I AM ME!" statement once said "I am a sinner" now I have added, "saved by grace". Feel free to include your relationship or lack thereof in your statement.

There are two purposes for the statement. (1) To provide you with a clear definition of yourself and the roles you play. Included is the knowledge of who you are to you, to other people, and to God. (2) To recognize your importance and begin to appreciate yourself. It is common to deal with low self-esteem and self-worth. When the mountain seems too difficult to climb, try a different route. Instead of immediately tackling self-esteem and self-worth issues, learn to appreciate yourself. After all, how can you esteem or assign worth to someone or something you yet to appreciate.

You are not stating whether or not you are a good mother or father. There is no room in this statement to critique the value of the relationships. You need to realize and understand your importance. You need to understand your "today". Yesterday you were only a few of the things in your statement. Today you are all those things. Tomorrow, you will me more!

# PART TWO:

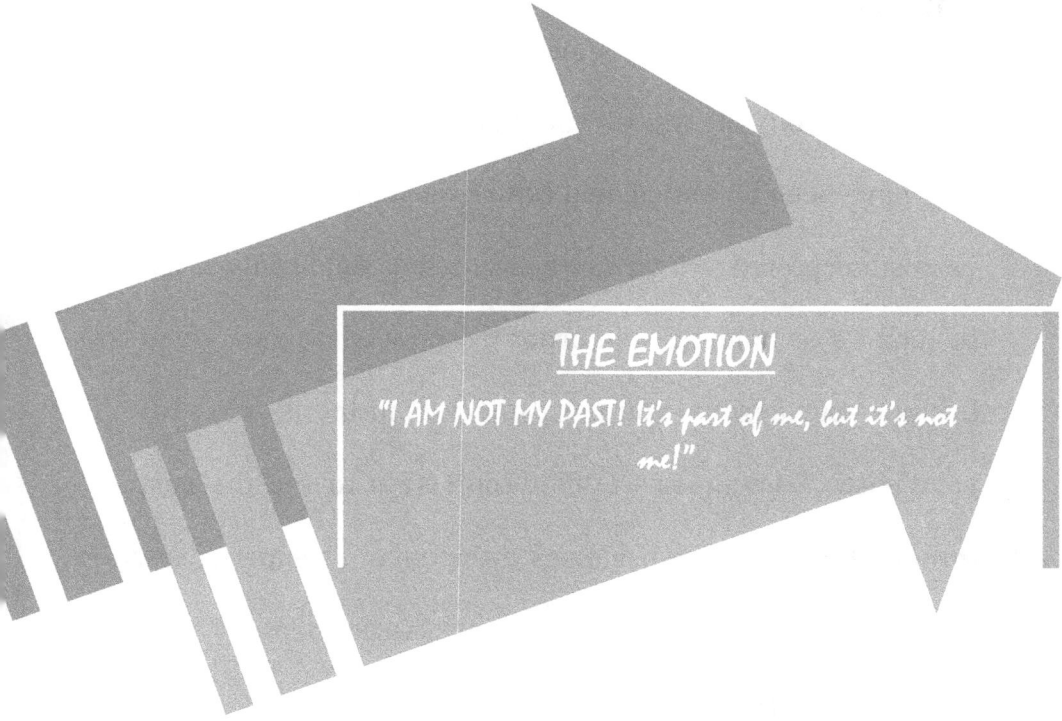

## THE EMOTION

*"I AM NOT MY PAST! It's part of me, but it's not me!"*

## Your Past

The past is what happened to you, around you, and because of you. It was at one time your present and even may have been an anticipated future moment. The past can be misinterpreted or improperly evaluated. But, it should not be ignored or hidden. In order to know who you are and live out your destiny, you must understand the purpose for your past. Sometimes we allow ourselves to see the past through the eyes of our feelings rather than as experiences. This hinders our understanding and assessment of past situations and relationships. What you endured (for better or worse) is meant to strengthen you and help others. You go through so you may pull others out. Your present is tomorrow's past. Is it that simple? Yes!

What was your past like? Did you hurt? Probably!

We are human. Hurt is a part of our humanity. Did you experience pleasures and joy? Of course, you did! What did you do with those moments? I hope you did not do like many and bury them under the hurts. I hope you did not consider those joyous moments as accessories to life. WAIT! Hurt and joy, those are emotions, feelings. They are not your past. Your past is the event which caused the emotions. Embrace the event.

The emotions of a painful event can create the feeling that one is a grasshopper instead of the mightiest of giants. Emotions can make us feel like we are the weakling in the situation when, in fact, we are the strong one. Clinging to emotion can make us see ourselves as right when in fact we are very wrong. These misperceptions keep us from apologizing to or forgiving others.

In your mind, take a step back into the events of your past. Look at them again. How did you feel? Now look at the event again. What happened? Put aside feelings and emotions and see what happened. Why did it happen? Who was involved? Once you can see a clear picture of the event (without pain, anger, or hurt), look at how it shaped you as a person. Be grateful for your past.

Let's look at me for a moment. I was raped more than once. Three times! At the age of twelve, I was raped by my best guy friend and his friend. They came to visit me at my families Plainsboro, NJ apartment. My best friend and his friend called earlier to ask if they could come play Nintendo with me. I told them they could come over. In a flash of a moment, I was stretched out on my parents' bed with a knife to my throat. They made me a woman, not allowing me the chance to be a lady. A part of me left with them as they exited my parent's bedroom window that night. I thought this was the worst thing that could ever happen to me.

The following year, my parents moved me to Orange,

NJ so my father could be closer to his church. I loved our apartment. I really liked my school. Until one day after spring break. I was thirteen. A tall, developing young woman with low self-esteem and no real understanding of sexuality was thrust into the world. The world proved its power. I was raped again! One year later! Only worse! I was battered, abused, assaulted, raped, and sodomized by three teenage boys in the Orange High School bathroom. As the guys were leaving, I asked, "Why did you do this to me?" (This was the same question I asked the boys in Plainsboro as the climbed out of the window. I still don't know why I asked either time.) They, almost in unison, responded. "Because you were there!" After two major surgeries and years of therapy, I was still not whole.

Life proceeded the way it should – as well as could be expected. My father, not understanding this as my testimony, called me names like tramp, whore, slut, harlot, street woman. As will be discussed later, the words of a parent are etched into a child's memory. There is no eraser that can make a child forget them. My mother, not understanding my internal struggle, thought I always had an attitude. My parents were otherwise loving and supportive people. They tried to understand and help. They loved me so much. I would not have survived without them.

But, there was another love I sought. I desperately looked for romantic, intimate love. I figured me saying "no" meant nothing. So, I manipulated myself into believing "yes" was my protector. Could it be said that I raped myself? Could it be I forced myself to have sex when I really did not want to? Could be.

I found what looked like love. I found a man. He was a few months younger than me. He was a real smooth talker. He was kinda cute too. I was 19. We laughed, talked, drank, smoked, and eventually lived together. Every once in a while, he would cheat on me. I cried. He apologized. We had sex. Every once and a while he would yell at me. I cried. He apologized. We had sex. Every once and a while he would hit me. I cried. He apologized. We had sex. Once I found out I was pregnant I knew life had gotten more serious than I could handle.

I wanted to leave him, but I was pregnant. (I was told after the second rape it would me very difficult or even near impossible to have children.) We got married six weeks after our son was born. Everyone said it was the thing to do – so I did it. He cheated on me on our wedding night! He cheated more. He hit me more. Our lives have little other memories except years of blackened eyes, swollen lips, and bitter tears.

After the birth of our second child, I knew this was too much. He had beaten me severely several times while I was pregnant which forced me to go to emergency doctor's appointments and into the hospital many times. At 3 years old, my oldest son looked at me, pulled my shirt, and said, "Mommy we need a new 'partment. No daddy." I left. When I returned to the apartment one day, I found him there with another woman. He and the woman held me down and pulled the braids out my head. I remember yelling but little else. I thought this was the worse life had to offer.

A few years later, I went to visit my father's cousin. She was a friend I needed in my life at the time. One summer day, she invited me to hang out. We went to a little lodge meeting hall which had a bar. I was twenty-six. I remember asking for an Absolute with cranberry. Things started getting hazy. I was always one to be able to hold my liquor. I had only been totally drunk twice and didn't like the feeling either time. This one drink felt like ten. The bartender, my father's cousin, and another guy suggested we go to a mansion party. Feeling like I was in no shape to drive, I figured "yes" was my only option.

As soon as I entered the rear of the house, I was pushed by someone into the pool. I couldn't swim! I eventually got out. Staggering around, I asked for a bathroom. I was pointed in the direction of a poolside restroom. Moments later I heard a knock at the door. I told the guy I would be out shortly. My mind was too foggy for me to realize I had not locked the door properly. A tall muscular man in a police uniform busted in. He pulled up my skirt, bent me over the sink (in the same manner as I was raped at thirteen) and took my love for myself. I was too numb to cry. It would be a long time before I would cry again. I felt worthless, used up, like nothing.

I tell you SOME of my story so you can know I lived this journey. So you can understand that I know what it is like to survive. To go through all of this – I felt alone. It would be a long time before I would cry again. But, that was my past. That was yesterday. Today, I am not grateful for the rapes. I am not grateful for the rapists. I am not grateful for the abuse at the hand of my then husband. But, I am grateful for my past which includes the rapes, rapists, abuse, and abusers. There is much more to my story. The events of my past have infused in me a strength I have been told not many people have.

My past has also given me the opportunity to speak with you by writing this book. Stepping out of the emotions of the past has allowed me to evolve. It is by taking out the pain; I can look back at the past, see its benefits, and grow beyond anger and blame. Being raped did not make me a better person. The struggle not to die as a result of the rape made me a better person. The journey from self-loathing to self-appreciation made me an asset rather than a liability to the future. Being beat by my husband did not make me a better woman. Fighting my way out of a murderous oppression and deadly depression, emerging as a lady of defined worth and Godly favor, is what made me better. I concentrate on the lesson, not the emotion. If I focused my thoughts, efforts, and attentions on how the people and events of the past made me feel. I would not be able to write to you, for you.

Am I saying you should not have emotions or feelings? NO! I am not saying that. Do not dwell there. Embrace your humanity! When you are going through what seems to be the worst time in your life, do not hide or bury your feelings. Identify your feelings, the cause, and the outcome (possible and probable). Do not spend your life assessing, come to a conclusion. Pull from the experiences.

I later learned much of my pain was at the hand or mouth of a pain filled man. Men hurt deep! Society does not allow them to cry in public. Society tells them to "man up". The result is generation upon generation of men with emotional, psychological, and spiritual hurts. Hurts which have no release. It was not acceptable for men to spend a day at the spa, until recently. What were they supposed to do? Am I justifying the rape and abuse of women? OF COURSE NOT! I am addressing a cause. A hurting man can be just as detrimental as a scorned woman. Women at times feel as though they own pain. After all, we birth children. We do not own pain. By belittling the intensity of a man's pain we are only feeding the fire. Men need to know it is okay to hurt so they can know it is okay to heal.

This is about looking at life through a rear view mirror. Ladies and gentlemen, you are looking ahead while keeping the past in your sights. Leave the anger, hurt, pain, and fear in the past along with the event. It is of no benefit to relive the emotions. See the past as a movie showing how you survived. After all, how can you survive your future unless you remember what you have already endured and lived through? When you face times where you feel you do not possess what it takes to live and strive on, glance in the rearview mirror. It is the same strength which brought you this far will get you through your current dilemma. You are probably stronger now than you were then. During the last obstacle, you had the opportunity to exercise your mental, emotional, and spiritual muscles.

You are more than the events and emotions of your past. The past is only one of many things which make up who you are today. You needed your past to make you. But, your past is not you!

# PART THREE:

## THE RESPONSIBILITY
### "I AM A CHILD, BUT I AM MORE!"

Many adults forget what it feels like to be a child. Children face many of the societal pressures we face as adults. To those pressures, they add being a child and having little to no say over their lives. Our words are what feed them. Whether encouraging or destructive, they are embedded into their memory. While children are trying to understand and discover who they are and will become, it is our words which echo in their heads. What words are you saying to your children and/or the children in your community?

Are the children around you fighting to be "something" when the words thrown at them are "you are nothing"? Have you ever told them their very existence makes it impossible for them to be a nothing or *a nobody*? Have you explained they are a unique creation empowered by God with talents and gifts which can change or improve lives?

"You are just like your mother/father!" This statement is often used to show negative attributes which are similar between a parent and child. It can cut to the very essence of a child. Are you showing the positive connections? Is that father a drug addict who also happens to be a great dancer? Have you told that child "you know you are a great dancer just like your father"? Or do you say, "You always slack off by dancing around **just like your father**"? It's about the child!

Single mothers, at times, can be known as "male bashers". Single fathers can be labeled, at times, as "disrespectful to women". Where do the children fit in? How can you effectively raise children to become *more* if you don't believe in their future as a lady or gentlemen? What are they to think of themselves if they constantly hear you talk down about the opposite sex? Men raising ladies and women raising gentlemen, pay attention to what you say. They can hear you and they definitely feel you.

I remember speaking to my ex-mother-in-law about my then husband's childhood. What I heard from her was shocking. I was too young to process it and run. She told me she hated having children. She never wanted boys and she didn't care if her sons knew it. A chill went through my body. She hugged me as she told me she loved me more than she loved her own sons. She did not realize what she had done.

I am thankful for the conversation on how not to be a mother. It was a conversation which taught me to look deeper than someone's actions. Could Sigmund Freud have been right? In this case, he probably was correct. The pain inflicted by a mother is a life-long pain. A male child (my husband) spent his life knowing he was unwanted. When he looked at me he could not understand my love. He thought the love of his mother, the hitting, yelling, and belittling, was love.

As a child grows, those negative statements (and many more than mentioned here) are woven into the fabric of every decision they make. Why is the power which we give these negative statements so great? Why is it seemingly true that the power of negative statements override the positive, nurturing compliments children receive during the course of their lives? I wonder if we learn to esteem ourselves or if we are born with self-esteem. I believe the former to be true. Book after book, article after article has been written on this topic.

For the purpose of this book, we will assume we were born neutral and with a "blank slate". Aristotle called it "tabula rasa" or inscribed tablet. John Lock called it the "blank slate". We will also assume we did not have a measurable level of self-esteem, nor were we born lacking self-esteem. According to the aforementioned gentlemen and my own beliefs, we were born on a quest. It is a quest to find out who we are, how special we are, and our overall worth to ourselves as defined by others. Understanding this, our minds are open and available. Some do not agree with the "blank slate" theory.

Now, about this "blank slate" – Let's delve ever so briefly into the world of handwriting analysis. It is known that when we are angry or otherwise excited in a negative manner our handwriting is deeply grooved into the paper. The expressions of our hearts are engraved on the page. Yet, when we are happy (joyous, calm, relaxed) our words flow freely, gliding, across the page. Other than the visible ink, there may be little to no impression left behind. Couldn't this be true of the "blank slate" – a child's mind? Couldn't it be true that we create a harsh groove with our negative, angry words scarring them for life? Take time to pay more attention to what you say to a child.

Make sure your positive, nurturing words do not just glide along the page of their mind. See to it your angry words are corrective and not destructive. You have the pen. You have the words. You have the responsibility to leave a positive lasting impression.

When I speak to my sons about their father, I purposely tell them the good things about him. I want them to understand I loved their father. They were not a mistake. They were the product of love. Even if the love was one-sided, my side, it was love. I tell them that while their father has negative traits, but so do I. There is no one perfect. I write excellence and greatness as gentlemen onto the slates of their minds.

By feeding positivity into my children, it helped me. How could I hate a man who gave me the greatest gift I have ever received? I am able to look at my children as a separate event in my past. They are not a part of the pain. They are my joy in the midst of all. I can smile. There is freedom in that thought. I love my children. My love is free from guilt, anger, resentment, or fear. It is love. I believe they can feel my love.

**Tell a child – "I know you are a child now, but you are more". Then help them become *more*.**

## "Who Am I?"

A person who has smarts

Who has strength and heart

A person who believes

I will succeed

With hopes that soar like a bird

Conquering the world word by word

They will yell my name

Education is my game

I have the knowledge

I will have a business after college

I am fulfilling my dreams

The sky has no limits it seems

A boy growing into a strong man

That is who I am!

TONISHA "DR. TONI" PINCKNEY

## By L. DaVante' Pinckney

### I AM A CHILD, BUT I AM MORE!

It's only been a short time since I was born

No one's quite sure how my life will take form

Some expect less of me because I'm too short or too tall

Some even say I will be nothing at all

They look at me and go blind by my color

Say I'm hopeless because of my father or mother

**I AM MORE!**


My heart is full of hopes and dreams

I just need someone on whose shoulder to lean

I am the strength of a future you can't ignore

The world is mine to fully explore

I am not limited by your words or your fears

I have become extraordinary in a few short years

I AM MORE: The Journey

## I AM MORE!

My legs will take me to amazing places

My eyes will look on prideful faces

How can you not see what I'm destined to be?

How can you look and not see what I see?

I will live to be excellent and strive for perfection

I will be set apart and not part of a collection

## I AM MORE!

Refer to me as lady or gentleman

Give me a platform on which to stand

Inspire me with love and respect

Be your best so your image I reflect

Show me the truth between right and wrong

Accept me even when I don't appear to belong

## I AM MORE!

I am strong when I feel weak

I will never profess defeat

I am brilliant not just smart

I am the Creator's work of art

I am the making of great success

I am to walk a life so blessed

**I AM A CHILD, BUT I AM MORE!**

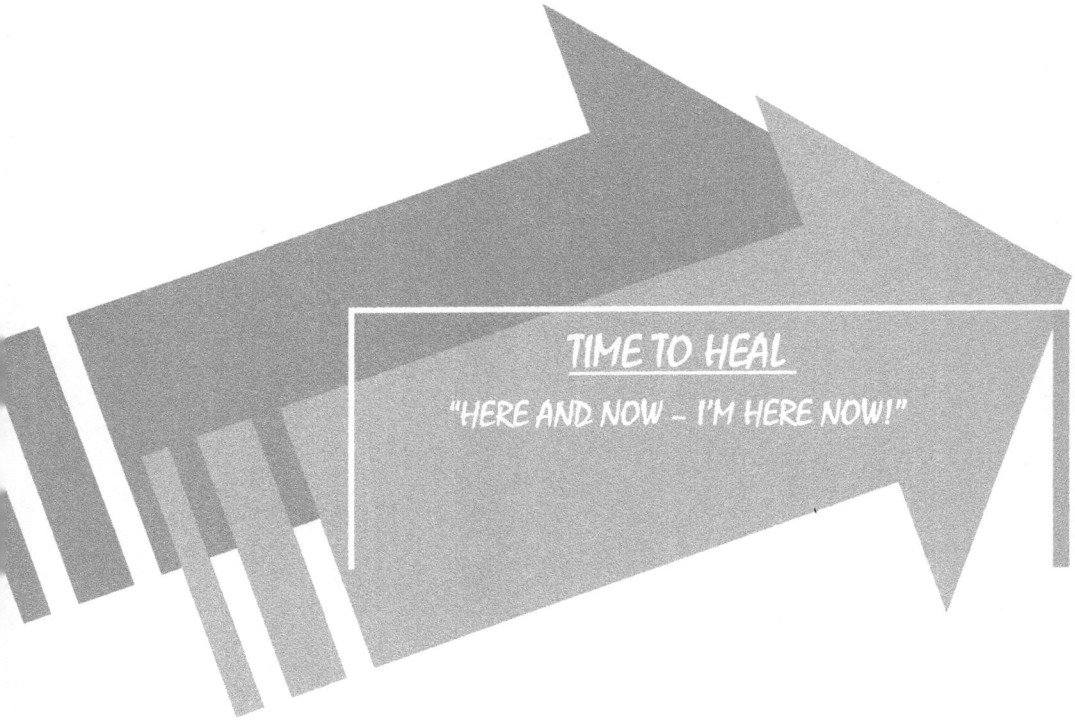

TIME TO HEAL
"HERE AND NOW – I'M HERE NOW!"

PART FOUR:

## NOW

You may not be proud of your past. You may have done things you are ashamed to think of and would never dare to say. What you have done or gone through may have caused your head to hang down. Your eyes may shift slightly to the left or right when speaking to someone because you know the things you have done. Hold your head up and look straight ahead. That person standing in front of you, the same person you are ashamed to speak to or in front of, may have images of a negative past hanging in their personal hall of shame.

Often times my past kept me from dating or even making new friends. I was scared to let anyone get close to me. If they got close they would learn me and about me. I was scared to be judged. I had made a lot of mistakes looking for love. I made more mistakes running from love. Who would understand? I could not understand; so, I thought it impossible for anyone else. My hall of shame was active in my mind. It was only after I put up the velvet rope and a sign saying "closed permanently" when I could let people into my life. It took time. It took time for me to realize closing the past (hall of shame) actually opened my future (my now).

Who are you now? Look again at your "I AM ME!" statement. You are even more than that. Insert aspects of your character. Are you strong? Honest? Loving? Caring? Those adjectives need to be in your statement. You need to see who you truly are to you. Receiving praise from others is a terrific experience. However, you must also praise yourself. Appreciate yourself. Society seems more focused on the concept of "what can you offer" your significant other, family, friends, and employer.

I dare you to look and see what you can offer yourself.

When there is no one around, can you give yourself what you need to go on in life? Determining what you have to offer yourself raises the quality of your life and empowers you to get through difficult moments. We all know the arrival of loneliness seems to coincide with the hardships of life. That is when you pull out your "I AM ME" statement, look at the events of the past (sans emotion), and see what you have already endured. I said to myself: "You are strong! You are trustworthy! You are a conqueror! You are at peace even in the worst times. You did it before! You survived!" If I was not in the past, I knew I evolved to become those things. You are here! Allow your survival to speak for itself.

Be truthful with yourself. If you are a liar – Say it! Put that in your statement. Have you stolen, cheated on a spouse, been in jail or prison, used drugs, or have you abused yourself or others? That must be a part of your statement. The *now* is that you are moving quickly away from it all. *Now* you are preparing to be more. You can't be more unless you know who you were and who you are now. Knowing who you are is not just about making yourself feel good. As part of my healing, I had to embrace my imperfections. Denial is only delayed pain. It is important to truly know your faults and limitations so you can grow, mature, and improve. The journey toward knowing yourself is not an ego trip!

THE POWER
"HE IS MORE, SO I AM MORE!"

# PART FIVE:

The purpose of this book is to empower you mentally, physically, emotionally, *and spiritually*. As life goes, this should be the first part of the journey. Unfortunately, most of us do not reach out to God or other power connections first. We choose to go our journey alone. So, I discuss this now. This is where God and power fit into my journey. Hopefully, when you are done reading, you will walk you journey putting God and this section first in your life. I do now, but I did not then.

In order to be empowered, we must be connected to a power source. I touched on this in an earlier chapter. So, where do you get this power? A dead battery can't charge itself. Connecting to people of social stature will inspire you. Mustering up courage, boldness, strength, and esteem will drive you. But, how do you succeed on the days when you feel you just can't go on? I am of the belief that placing yourself in a position to connect with God will empower you. It is actually quite liberating when you connect to the power source who is God.

There is freedom in knowing you are not taking the full responsibility for deciding your future. There is a peace in not relying on other imperfect creations (people) to direct your path. There is hope in knowing there is a purpose for all which has happened to you. There is power in realizing the eye which sees all, the ear which hears all, the heart which loves all, the arms that protect all, the knowledge that teaches all, and the power that empowers all is your source.

The entire Bible is meant to give direction. There is not a single aspect of your life which God (through the Bible) has not given you a path to follow. He (God) knows your tomorrow when it is still yesterday. When others have placed limitations on your life – He is more so you are more. When you look in the mirror and see the scars from an abusive mother, father, husband, wife, or child – He is more so you are more. You do not have to be more by yourself. You do not have to carry the burden alone. I wish I would have realized sooner.

We must be realistic! Our yesterdays seem to follow us. Many say, "My past is forever before me". Stop giving so much power to your past. In the latter portion of Genesis 19:17 (NIV) it says: "Flee for your lives! Don't look back, and don't stop anywhere in the plain! Flee to the mountains or you will be swept away!" If you feel your past is forever before you – then you need to turn around! QUICK! You are facing the wrong way! Look up to God and live. You are giving too much power to your past! We spend so much time looking back at the past we become swept away by the emotions and the pain of the past.

I encourage you to run to the mountains (look to the hills) where you will find help. Face God and turn your back to the past. Flee for your life. Allow pain to die so you may live. The winds of the past are holding you back or, at the very least, slowing you down. BUT, if you turn around, putting your back to the past, those winds meant to hinder you will become the very force pushing you forward.

There are people around who will constantly remind us of our shortcomings. They convince us (intentionally or not) the prospect of our greatness was destroyed. That was yesterday. Take back the power you have given those who were the spectators of your past. You live by disconnecting from people meant to drain your power. You live by connecting to the source of your power – God.

It is so easy for us to embrace our sinful nature. It is true we were born sinful. We have certain undesirable attitudes and behaviors we inherited from our parents. Some of us had to grow up and live in environments which fostered these negative attributes. I challenge you to understand there is more to you. The journey for me was in 4 steps: (1) He (God) is I AM that I AM (2) I am me (3) He is more so (4) I am more. I had to first recognize the attributes of God before I could clearly see the positive attributes I possessed. I focused too much on the sin that dwelled within. The constant rehashing the thought of myself as a sinner prevented me from seeing God's grace.

As we continue to assess our past and its role in the future, many of us realize a new beginning is needed. We need to assign a moment and say, "My life starts over riiiiight now!" Let's talk about creation - Genesis 1:1 – "In the beginning God created the heaven and the earth." Ok, so "In the beginning God created"... Now John 1:1, 2- "In the beginning was the Word, and the Word was with God, and the

Word was God. The same was in the beginning with God." – Ok, so "in the beginning God created" and "in the beginning was the Word which was with God and was God and was in the beginning". So God and the Word which was both God and with God were there in the beginning but at some point created. I said this to say God can choose any point He wants to create.

Since He is the beginning of the thing because He is the creator of the thing He can create the thing anytime He wants. So if He (God who creates) created you and the time continuum in which you exist, can He not create a new beginning at any point? **Are you waiting for a healing when God is speaking creation?** Is it not feasible that He (God who creates) who created the beginning in the first can create a new beginning for you not dependent on time or circumstance? Is it not feasible that HE (God the Word who was there at your creation and exists independent of all that is created) can speak the Word of new life and creation into your spirit anytime you need it.

Because God can create a new beginning at any point, because He can bring completion at any time because he can create a new you without the restraints of time and space MEANS the possibilities of who you can become are infinite. We hear about the attributes of God in church all the time. We sing about them. He's a provider, He's a way maker, He is all-powerful, and He is all knowing. How great is our God? His name is excellent in all the earth. He is Alpha and Omega. He is Merciful. He is Wonderful. And so on and so on.

Who does God say He is? For this let 's look at semi-familiar scripture, **Exodus 3:13-14** "And Moses said unto God, Behold, when I come unto the children of Israel, and shall say unto them, The God of your fathers hath sent me unto you; and they shall say to me, What is his name? what shall I say unto them? [This is the same as saying God who should I tell them you are?] And God said unto Moses, I AM THAT I AM: and he said, Thus shalt thou say unto the children of Israel, I AM hath sent me unto you."

I want you to get this. God could have said I am God and there is no other. He could have said I am the creator of all. He could have said anything to describe Himself and say who He is and was. But He chose to say I AM that I AM! In other words, God Himself recognized He was *more* than can be put into words. In other words, I AM ALL the mind can comprehend and more. He was saying: "there is nothing that I AM not" because I AM that I AM. HE IS MORE! He is so much more He Himself could not label Himself. God Himself expressed how infinite He is by simply saying I AM that I AM.

How does this connect to your life? Well, He (God) dwells in you, right? You ARE His temple – right? You *are* a vessel available to Him – Right? Ok God is great – He is in me/you – meaning greatness is in me/you. God is excellent –

I AM MORE: The Journey

He is in me/you – meaning excellence is in me/you. God is strength – so holiness must be in me/you. God is a creator – so we have the ability to create and carry life. God is powerful – so I/we possess power. He is a protector, so since I have a protector in me, I as a lady have the ability to protect my children. He is a lily in the valley – so I have the ability to be a source of both beauty and strength standing tall in the deepest darkest situation. Are you feeling me on this – He is more so I am more? God is faithful. So the next time you are faced with the decision whether to cheat on a test or a companion, remember God is in you so faithfulness is in you. While you can obtain levels of greatness without a connection to God, you will not reach the pinnacle of greatness.

Stop trying to pursue the very attributes you had from birth. Stop trying to be great. You are great – walk in your greatness. Why waste time saying you are trying to become more? You are more – live it! Just as you were, admittedly so by most, born with the propensity to commit wrong and evil acts, you were also born with the overwhelming ability to overcome. You were born great. You were born *more*.

---

## HE IS MORE, SO I AM MORE!

Yesterday you saw my ending

But God said it was the beginning

Yesterday you saw my withering hope

But God helped me cope

Yesterday you cast me aside

But God sent a Comforter to abide

**He is More, So I AM MORE!**

Yesterday you showed your disdain

But God promised to transform my pain

Yesterday you waved your hand and turned your face

But God showed me my exalted place

Yesterday you ignored the obvious

I AM MORE: The Journey

But God called me virtuous

**He is More, So I AM MORE!**

Yesterday, you reminded me of my yesterday

But God gave me a yesterday called today

Yesterday you told me my nothing was everything

But God said your everything was nothing

Yesterday you told me my limit

But God sent me His Spirit

**He is More, So I AM MORE!**

I am a daughter of the Most High

I am free to move hands untied

His strength is my strength indeed

He supplies for my every need

I am a product of perfection

I am resurrected through resurrection

**He is More, So I AM MORE!**

I know the intent of my Father

I rest in His love so I never tire

I am the epitome of excellence

He folds me into his presence

His has never let me walk alone

I bow humbly at His throne

**He is More, So I AM MORE!**

I reverence the Creator of all that is

My heart desires to pleasure His

My soul looks to His wondrous Grace

I found in Him my healing place

He knew my future before I became your past

I am set apart not an outcast

**He is More, So I AM MORE!**

My eyes saw the reflection of my damage

His eyes saw the creation of His image

I can try my best but still transgress

He is everything and nothing less

I AM MORE: The Journey

He is my love my hope my peace

I know His power so I decrease

**He is More, So I AM MORE!**

By His authority I have power

**He is More, So I AM MORE!**

By His Word my sin has closure

**He is More, So I AM MORE!**

By His blood I have redemption

**He is More, So I AM MORE!**

By His mercy my life has direction

**He is More, So I AM MORE!**

By His love, I can love

**He is More, So I AM MORE!**

By His wisdom, I am certain of...

**He is More, So I AM MORE!**

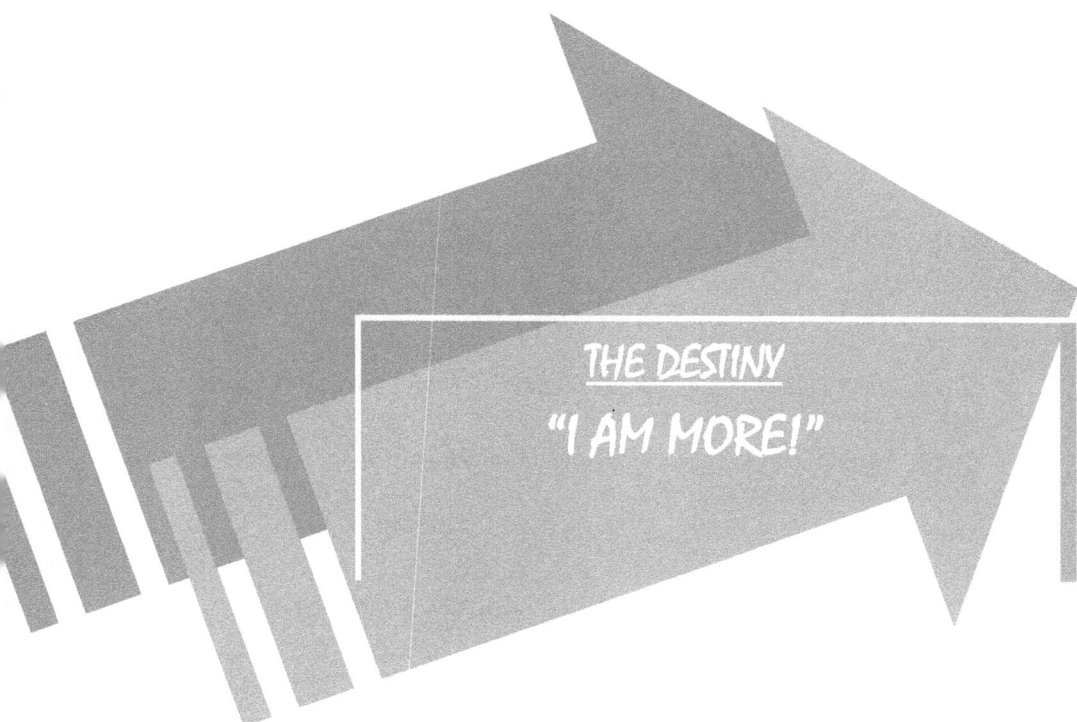

THE DESTINY

"I AM MORE!"

PART SIX:

## I AM MORE!

Once today is over, it will be the past. Do not take the worries and troubles of today into tomorrow. Isn't it enough you had to deal with it for one day? *TRUST THAT TODAY IS NOT AN EXTENSION OF YESTERDAY, NOR IS IT A PREVIEW OF TOMORROW - TODAY IS JUST TODAY - GOOD OR BAD - TODAY IS the ONLY MOMENT BY MOMENT.* Trust More! Trust God More! Trust Yourself More! Trust the Vision More! Trust Your Dream More!

More. More. More. What does it mean to be more? Does wanting to be more mean the way you are now is not good enough? Why is being more so important? The best part about always seeing yourself as *more* is there is no "the end" in view. Dreams become visions that turn into realities, which births new dreams, that become new visions, then new realities that...well, you get it. Once you stop believing there is *more* to you and in you, the cycle ends.

Situations and circumstances of life have the tendency to take charge if we are not careful. We can fall into the black hole of hopelessness and complacency. Once we realize our circumstances are not who or what we are, we can grow into the concept of being 'more". Stop being restricted by your situation. Change your view. See the batterer, abuser, smooth talker, trifling woman, poverty, illness, and any other painful moment as what it is meant to be. It is a tool to strengthen you and the catalyst making you into the person you are predestined to be.

It took me 31 years to realize that I was more. I had given negativity the power to define me. I forgot I was shaped by God. I thought it was everything that happened to and around me that formed who I was and who I was to become. The image floating in my head called my past, is not me! It was then that I prayed a very simple prayer, "Lord, allow me to see life, people, and everything through your eyes". It was in the days following when realized "I am more". Just like you, I was made in God's image. I began to imagine ("image in") myself as a reflection of His image. And, because of who God is, "He is more, so I am more".

As you look in the mirror of your mind, clear the image of you. Forget what you see. Then look again. Look at who your parents raised. Erase that image. Imagine "the who" you dreamed you would be. Delete that. Picture nothing. If you were told you would be nothing or nobody – they were wrong. Understand that "nothingness" in itself is impossible. The very vision of nothing is impossible. The fact of your existence is the very image/proof you are more. Imagine (IMAGE IN) that! To believe you are nothing or "a nobody" is to believe you do not exist. But, the very fact that you can think, feel, see, and understand proves you exist. You are the greatness that is you. That is what you need to "image in". You are the perfectly formed image of God and designed by Him - you are more.

After I began to appreciate myself and God for making me, the mother part of my mind immediately thought of the children. I looked at my children, the children playing in the street, and thought about the ones running from gunshots or trying to escape the murderous words of oblivious parents. I wanted all those babies to say "I am a child, but I am more".

I thank God for every new day. Every day is an opportunity to be more than what I ever thought. For each new day puts my past further behind and my destiny even closer. It is a step into my future. Every yesterday is a part of my testimony to the greatness of God and finding the strength to survive. I define "tomorrow" as the hope that changes the definition of my past. For when tomorrow becomes yesterday - I believe my past will no longer be a testament to tears. When tomorrow becomes yesterday, I will call my past blessed. In order to fully step into and be blessed by your future, you must understand the purpose of your past. This is where you will find your past does not have power over you. The purpose of your past is to make you more.

One day, I was about to cry one of those really hard and loud cries. Not only had I lost my job and car, my son was hospitalized three hundred miles away, my lights were out, and the landlord knocked on my door with a final notice of eviction letter. This all happened within a six-week time span. Then, I remembered, I really am more! My God really is more! So, since He is more than the events which brought me to the verge of tears - I am more! The tears formed as an expression of pain - fell as an expression of praise and worship. I lived the ""I AM ME" to I AM MORE!" process. I learned to keep living the process.

Ladies, you are more than the sex you can give. Gentlemen, you are more than your sexual conquests. Ladies and gentlemen of all ages, you are more than the pain or praise attached to these meaningless accomplishments.

I spent so much time - wasted time - trying to configure my life (or what I thought was the plan for my life) based on the past, words of outsiders, and my current circumstances. I could not see beyond. I was blinded by the idea of being. I was so consumed with the need to connect my self-worth to success that I failed to realize that I was already a success – I was already full of value and worth. Instead, I now live the concept of being more. I could say "I am more than rape" or "I am more than domestic violence" or "I am more than a preacher's kid" or "I am more than a graduate". But, by connecting being more to an event (using the word "than") I am still limiting myself. In this case, complexity is found in simplicity. I AM MORE can be attributed to every thought positive and negative. In every emotion, I AM MORE. In every situation, whether it is for the best or the worse, I AM MORE.

You must understand - within the realization of being *more* lives the spirit of excellence. You are to strive for excellence and trust God for perfection. He (God) is more, so you (in whatever state) are more. Because He is perfect, you can be perfected. Because God is all-knowing, you can have knowledge. Because He (God) is loving, you can be loved and give love. Because God is God, you can be more. His plan for you is limitless. There are no boundaries. As humans we have boundaries. Our vision can only extend so far. Our dreams are always followed by "the end". So in order to see beyond, in order to be *more*, we must look to the very God who created us.

The prayer of Jabez in I Chronicles 4:10 of the Bible says, "Oh, that you would bless me and enlarge my territory!"

Don't we all want an enlarged territory? Of course, we do. The challenge here is the step you take prior to the prayer. You have to first enlarge your mental territory before asking God to enlarge your physical territory. You need to expand your thinking to include all and limit nothing. Limited thinking leads to limited faith and choices.

Enlarge the territory of your mind/thinking so you can see past the now. There is a chance God may have already expanded your territory. But, due to the limitations YOU have placed on your thinking, you are blinded to the vastness of YOUR territory. Do you have enough faith to know that everywhere you stand, everywhere you go, and everyone you meet is meant to be part of your territory? We are all players on one another's expansion teams. We are all meant to grow, connect, and expand the territory of our community, church, family, and country.

Now go back into your mind. Envision, "image in",

who you are. See who you are not. See yourself clearly. You are more than that! You are an ever improving creation. Every minute you are more than the minute before. Every day you have the opportunity to be more than the greatest moment of your past. Year by year you grow mentally, physically, psychologically, and spiritually into more, and more, and more. Man, woman, boy, and girl: Proclaim to yourself - 'I AM MORE!"

# I Am More!

Yes my legs are long as time

But never you mind

Yes my lips are full and supple

But you're not worth the trouble

You see me as the epitome of sexuality

A living breathing novelty

**I am more!**

Yes my breast will fill your manly hands

But I need you to take two steps back and stand

Yes my eyes are wide and my eyelashes long

But you must realize we sing a different song

You see me as the lips that pleasure

A mere fulfillment of your leisure

I AM MORE: The Journey

**I am more!**

Yes my hands can massage away a month's worth of pain

But I ask you to refrain

Yes my hips sway from east to west

But to you, I am far less

You see me as the hope of an evening

A memory not worth retrieving

**I am more!**

I am a lady full of desire

I have dreams no one can retire

My lips kiss the hopes of my children

For the future, I hold the banner and sound the siren

My arms carry the weight of my household

My legs stride the lengths of painful trails untold

**I am more!**

TONISHA "DR. TONI" PINCKNEY

I am a lady that has survived those like you

With wisdom, I made the decision to breathe through

My mind entices the prospects of education

I am appropriate in every situation

I am that glass of unsipped wine

I wait silently for my time

**I am more!**


I am the lady that lights a room

I am prepared for my future groom

My strengths grew from past weakness

I am the epitome of uniqueness

My tongue speaks words from the Book of Life

My teeth house the mutterings of unspeakable strife

**I am more!**

I am the lady who hears from God

I AM MORE: The Journey

I walk with a mare's graceful trod

My thoughts exceed the here and now

My eyes seek those who forgot to be found

My soul receives the Creator's message

I have been freed from bondage

**I am more!**

To know who I am you must know my Creator

**I am more!**

To understand me you must know my desire

**I am more!**

To love me you must feel my pain

**I am more**

To have me you must know the ground I seek to regain

**I am more**

To be with me you must see through God's eyes

**I am more!**

To become one you must know, understand, and love...

**I am more!**

## *Standing Strong, I AM MORE!*

You see a father absent from a chosen generation

I stand a man penning a child's future navigation

You see the cries of a lonely mother

I stand a son, husband, father, and brother

You see the end of a promised dream

I stand the source of wisdom from which your children will glean

**Standing Strong, I AM MORE!**


You look to me with little expectation

I stand in a place of preparation

You refuse to look past the love of my soul

I stand through it all remarkably bold

You see eyes filled with anger, hurt, and pain

I AM MORE: The Journey

I stand seeing the tools I use for my destiny to regain

**Standing Strong, I AM MORE!**

Arms extended well beyond their natural length

Nostrils flared, tickled by life's stench

A crown of mockery forced upon my head

Grabbing and piercing my flesh are the angry words you said

A generational curtain between you and I

Holding back, I refuse to cry

**Standing Strong, I AM MORE!**

You followed me declaring your praise

Standing behind me planning the end of my days

The weight of your disapproval threatens to break my back

The bitterness of my image overshadows your lack

The silence of your love deafens me

Your footsteps trod through the rivers of my expectancy

## Standing Strong, I AM MORE!

Society's mission is to destroy the value of my name

Replacing my glory with useless fame

Transforming my sweat into drops of blood

Forcing my knees into pools of mud

A slowing death perched for all to see

Thunderous applause forces the hope of painful eternity

**Standing Strong, I AM MORE!**

A man of powerful intensity and strength

**Standing Strong, I AM MORE!**

A man willing to bend, but will never be broken

**Standing Strong, I AM MORE!**

A man who protects the weakened protector

**Standing Strong, I AM MORE!**

A man whose present will be gifted not taken

**Standing Strong, I AM MORE!**

A man handcrafted in the image of Perfection

**Standing Strong, I AM MORE!**


Integrity

    Vision

        Loyalty

            Principle

                Power

What was meant for my ending is resurrected as my beginning.

**Standing Strong, I AM MORE!**

# PART SEVEN:

## THE JOURNEY

FROM: "I AM ME!"     TO     "I AM MORE!"

## Journey

### "I Am Me" to "I AM MORE"

Welcome to a process designed to usher you into a place of appreciation for yourself, your past, your faith, and your community.

In this section, you will write and re-write the book of your life. You will have the opportunity to mark a single day as the dividing line between your past and your future. Today will truly be today, and not just an extension of the past. Hopefully, you will remember the event(s) affecting you most. Then attempt to leave behind the residue of the emotions and fears associated with it. You will address these residual emotions which impacted your present and, up until now, future in a negative way. I also hope you will recall the lessons from previous chapters, and positive character traits gained when identifying the negative attributes by name and their source.

You will assess and re-assess your life. Even though it is labeled as a 4-week journey it is really an 8-week journey (two 4-week journeys). Each day there is a thought, focus, and challenge. At the end of each, you will see a "greater challenge" which is *not* to be completed during the first 4-week cycle. At the end of the 4 weeks, you are to go back to day one. Using what you have learned about yourself over the first cycle, you are to re-read the thoughts, focuses, and challenges. This time, you are to complete the "greater challenge". The journey is meant to introduce you to yourself and remind you of your inner strength.

Like life, you do not realize what you have learned while you are still living the experience. After you look back and assess the journey you can clearly see the lessons learned. The same is true of the journey in this section of the book. The first 4-week trip you will discover truths about you, your past, and your connections. The second trip will allow you to read what you wrote, analysis it, and add to it through the greater challenge.

You may not fill up all the lines on the first cycle – no worries. It is also okay to take longer than 4 weeks per cycle. It is just fine to skip portions (even though it is not encouraged or suggested). You may want to take a day or two extra to reflect and think. Try to write more than one answer. DO NOT go on to the next day until you are comfortable you have internalized what you wrote. Know who you are, what you are more than, and how to connect the purpose of your past to the path of your future.

The journey starts with you writing your "I Am Me" statement(s) and climaxes with your "I AM MORE" statement(s). The journey is circular. As mentioned in the preceding pages, you cannot truthfully say "I AM MORE" until you are comfortable saying "I Am Me". This is not a psychological journey to wellness. It is simply becoming intimate with you. It is a journey I took. I didn't have a book or guide (other than the Bible) to take me on this journey. To you, it will hopefully bring self-awareness, self-worth, self-esteem, and a strong sense of faith and spirituality. Ultimately, your goal is to learn how to esteem and treat you! Then you can be healthy (mentally) when esteeming others.

Others will see *you* which you are transmitting. Like a satellite signal, others pick up only on what is transmitted. That is the information they process and the information they use to base all future interactions. It's time to learn what you are transmitting so you may relay the proper information, to the proper people, at the proper time, and in the proper manner.

God bless and good journey to you! Allow me to introduce you to a spectacular, extraordinary, strong, talented, focused, bold, mature, and confident person **– YOU!**

## WEEK ONE

## DAY ONE

**Thought:** Today, _____ (write date) is day one. It is the marker separating the past from the future. Every event is in the past, and with it is every emotion linked to it.

**Focus:** Healing, Strength, Life

**Challenge:** Begin writing your "I AM ME!" statement. List the events you have endured in a way which shows your strength. The challenge is not to relive the emotion, but to acknowledge your strength.

>   Ex:  I am a survivor of abuse – "I AM ME"!

>   I conquered anger – "I AM ME"!

---

_____

_____

_____

_____

_____

_____

_____

_____

**Greater Challenge: Where do you find the spiritual source of your strength?**

_____

_____

_____

_____

_____

_____

_____

## WEEK ONE

## DAY TWO

**Thought:** Continue the journey toward releasing the hindering powers of your past. One way to do this is by assessing the various roles you play or have played in the lives of others. You are somebody who is unique and special.

**Focus:** Healing, Relationships, Individuality

**Challenge:** Write the next line(s) of your "I AM ME!" statement. List the roles you have played in the lives of others. It does not matter if they were simple or complex. The challenge is to not concentrate on whether or not you succeeded in those roles.

Ex: I am a son, father, friend – "I AM ME"!

I am a woman – "I AM ME"!

_____

_____

_____

_____

_____

_____

_____

_____

**Greater Challenge: Which relationships had the greatest success?                                        Why?**

_____

_____

_____

_____

_____

_____

TONISHA "DR. TONI" PINCKNEY

## WEEK ONE

## DAY THREE

**Thought:** You are no longer product of your past – You are a facilitator of your future. Concentrate on how you can change the stumbling blocks of the past into tools for the future.

**Focus:** Finding strength and assessing power

**Challenge:** Delve a little deeper into the next layer of your "I AM ME!" statement. List the positive attributes you used to become who you are today. The challenge is to know that: Despite the events of your past you are...

Ex: I am strong, peaceful, calm, and bold – "I AM ME"!

I am learning, maturing – "I AM ME"!

_____

_____

TONISHA "DR. TONI" PINCKNEY

_____

_____

_____

_____

_____

_____

**Greater Challenge: What negative attributes are you carrying forward from the past?**

_____

_____

_____

_____

_____

_____

_____

## WEEK ONE

## DAY FOUR

**Thought:** Today's journey is to go from just existing as a man or a woman to becoming a lady or a gentleman. The mere mention of the term "lady" or "gentleman" conjures up definite images. (Images of sophistication, stature, and certain poise.) "Image in" that and carry yourself as such.

**Focus:** Image to "Image In"

**Challenge:** Write in your "I AM ME!" statement a description of the lady or gentleman you imagine (image in) yourself to be. The challenge is not to portray an image of what you have endured or acquired, but who you are inside. "Image in"

Ex: I am a lady of sophistication and wisdom –

I am a gentleman of distinction and power –

_____

                                          **"I AM ME"!**

_____

_____

_____

_____

_____

_____

_____

_____

**Greater Challenge: Change your appearance to align with**

**what        you        "Image        in".**

_____

_____

_____

_____

_____

_____

I AM MORE: The Journey

_____

_____

_____

_____

_____

_____

_____

_____

_____

_____

_____

_____

_____

**WEEK ONE**

## DAY FIVE

**Thought:** Re-read what you have written from day one until now. Think about what questions arose when reflecting on your statements. You are getting to know you!

**Focus:** Healing and self-assessment

**Challenge:** Look at the ""I AM ME" statement as it is. What do you think you need to add or re-word to more positively reflect your true self? Do NOT subtract anything. Write what you have learned about yourself so far.

---

_____

_____

_____

_____

_____

_____

_____

_____

_____

**Greater Challenge: Address the "I AM" issues which are hindering your progress. How can they push you forward rather than hinder you?**

_____

_____

_____

_____

_____

_____

_____

_____

TONISHA "DR. TONI" PINCKNEY

_____

_____

_____

_____

_____

_____

_____

_____

_____

_____

_____

**WEEK ONE**

**DAY SIX**

**Thought:** Your "I AM ME!" statement is almost complete. Gifts and talents are a part of you – a very important part. You will be happier and more at peace when you exercise those gifts and talents. But, you must first identify them.

**Focus:** Self-Worth, Gifts, Talents

**Challenge:** In your "I AM ME!" statement add you gifts/talents as absolutes. Do not say, "I write poetry". Say, "I am a poet". The challenge is to continue to re-define you by adding gift/talents.

_____

_____

_____

_____

_____

_____

_____

_____

_____

_____

**Greater Challenge: Which of your gifts/talents are you not utilizing to their fullest? How can you change this?**

_____

_____

_____

_____

_____

_____

_____

_____

_____

**WEEK ONE**

## DAY SEVEN

**Thought:** You have spent the last six days (maybe more) of this journey focusing on you. Come up for air. This is the day you give yourself a rest from analyzing yourself, identifying life changing events, and displaying your gifts/talents.

**Focus:** Rest, Relax, Relationships

**Challenge:** Take today to connect differently with someone in your life. Compliment something about them which seems to go unnoticed. Document their response. The challenge is to see how powerful a positive attitude is in a relationship. Keep your notes short – today is supposed to be a break!

_____

_____

_____

_____

TONISHA "DR. TONI" PINCKNEY

_____

_____

_____

_____

_____

_____

**Greater Challenge: Positively affect the lives of 5 people with your words. What did you say?**

_____

_____

_____

_____

_____

_____

_____

## **WEEK TWO**

During week one, you wrote your "I AM ME!" statement. You should have a healthier more grounded image of yourself. You should be able to "image in" yourself in a new way.

But, you have not yet dealt with your past. You have merely identified the past events as they have happened. You have not expressed the emotions attached to the events. You have not yet embraced the purpose of any painful events or unjustifiably joyous happenings.

This may be a rough week for some. However, you must remember your past is not always about you. You will be on a journey which (hopefully) helps you to identify how your past has equipped you to help others. By going through, you should now know what it takes to help pull someone out. Be careful not to fall into the trap of re-living the past in such a way that you sink into sadness or even depression. Do not be swept away by your emotions. You have already lived through your past. You should now be strong enough to deal with it and leave the emotions there. This is a healing process. Know you are ripping the bandage off the wound so you can heal without infection and with minimal scarring. The healing process is not complete until you understand how you got hurt, how to avoid placing yourself in the position to sustain the same hurt, and to help others who are experiencing or have experienced similar pain.

Turn your back on the past and look towards your future. Draw from the lessons learned and strengths gained. You possess a strength not had by all. Remember that strength as you go through this week. I pray for your continued strength.

If you need to, write your "I AM ME!" statement from week one on a separate sheet of paper for you to reference at the end of each day's challenge.

Have a blessed continuation of your journey. Be

prepared to discover what you like or dislike about yourself.

Most importantly, find the true you on the other end.

**Again, you are no longer a product of your past; you are a facilitator of your future!**

## WEEK TWO

### DAY ONE

**Thought:** The emotions of the past hinder our future success more than the event that triggered the emotion. It is important to access memories as they are before attempting to interpret or analyze them. Again, this is not a psychological journey, it is a soul journey.

**Focus:** Healing

**Challenge:** Write out the complete narrative of an event that negatively changed your life. Be clear. Be real. The challenge is to say how you felt before, during, and after - identifying all your emotions (positive and negative). Stay focused on the event, though.

*If there is more than one event, only cover one event per week*

## Greater Challenge: Assess the significance of the event sans emotion.

_____

_____

_____

_____

_____

_____

_____

_____

_____

_____

_____

_____

## WEEK TWO

## DAY TWO

**Thought:** We change, and things change us, for the better or worse. Go back in time to before the event you wrote about above. Who were you then? It is not good enough to just know what happened. In order to move forward, you must know how it affected you and/or changed the course of your life.

**Focus:** Memory, Emotion, Heal

**Challenge:** Re-read your full "I AM ME!" statement. Looking back at who you were before that life-changing event, did you leave anything out? Is there something (positive or negative) about you that has been forgotten or ignored? If yes, write it down. If no, why are you so sure?

_____

_____

_____

_____

_____

_____

_____

**Greater Challenge: Write out an "I AM ME!" statement as it would have looked before this event. Ponder the change.**

_____

_____

_____

_____

_____

_____

_____

## WEEK TWO

## DAY THREE

**Thought:** Unfortunately, life sometimes happens for the worse not better. Regardless of how big or small the event, negative traits can be embedded in us. For example, we could lose our sense of strength or gain a degree of bitterness. To move forward, let's identify those traits.

**Focus:** Embrace, Heal

**Challenge:** Avoid walking into your future dragging along the residue of the past. Those positive traits you lost and negative traits you gained are unnecessary reminders of pain. Identify what died, or has been born in you, as the result of your actions or an event.

_____

_____

_____

_____

_____

_____

_____

_____

_____

_____

**Greater Challenge: Write in order of importance the undesired feelings, emotions, or traits born in you as a result of the event.**

_____

TONISHA "DR. TONI" PINCKNEY

_____

_____

_____

_____

_____

_____

_____

_____

_____

_____

_____

_____

_____

_____

_____

_____

_____

---

## WEEK TWO

## DAY FOUR

**Thought:**  Forgiveness is a powerful action.  It requires that the person forgiving separate the action from the person that caused it. It may be impossible to forgive a rape, murder, or abuse, but it is definitely possible to forgive the rapist, murderer, or abuser.  Your healing is trapped behind the doors of forgiveness

**Focus:** Forgiveness, Healing

**Challenge:**  List people that have abused, hindered, or in any way hurt you.  You may even have to list yourself as a hindrance. What is preventing you from forgiving them? It is not necessary for them to be around or confronted in order to be forgiven by you.

---

_____

_____

_____

_____

_____

_____

_____

_____

**Greater Challenge:   Identify your role in the event. Forgive                                    yourself.**

_____

_____

_____

_____

I AM MORE: The Journey

---

---

---

---

---

---

---

---

---

---

---

---

---

---

---

---

## WEEK TWO

## DAY FIVE

**Thought:** Painful events have residual affects/effects. While we are processing our feelings and emotions, we may (by chain reaction) cause a painful event in the life of another. OR, we may have been so self-aware that we used our pain to help another.

**Focus:** Heal to Heal

**Challenge:** Assess your attitude before and after the event. How did it affect others? Were you able to help or did you hurt? In order to become more, you must begin to identify the effect you have on the lives of others.

_____

_____

_____

_____

_____

**Greater Challenge: Develop a plan or way you could actively help heal someone (or the community) based upon your own painful events and experiences. (You do not have to know of anyone at the moment.)**

_____

_____

_____

_____

_____

_____

## WEEK TWO

## DAY SIX

**Thought:** In the preceding chapters, I spoke of being swept away by emotion. Sometimes the walk into the future feels as if we are fighting against a strong wind. We have the winds of emotion before us. Turn your back to the wind. Use the wind to thrust you ahead rather than hold you back.

**Focus:** Emotions, Healing, Power

**Challenge:** Identify the emotions you have allowed to be the wind in your face sweeping you toward your past rather than pushing you into your destiny.

_____

_____

_____

_____

_____

_____

_____

_____

_____

_____

_____

**Greater Challenge:** "Image In" and reflect on who you would have been if it were not for that space in time (the event).

_____

_____

_____

_____

_____

_____

TONISHA "DR. TONI" PINCKNEY

_____

_____

_____

_____

_____

_____

_____

_____

_____

_____

_____

_____

_____

_____

---

## WEEK TWO

## DAY SEVEN

**Thought:** Empowerment requires a source of power. Family, God, Education, Religious Organizations, etc. are sources of power. Make sure you are connected to the right power source for YOUR life.

**Focus:** Spirituality, Healing, Power

**Challenge:** Read the poem "He Is More, So I am More" again. (You may need to pray a little *wink*). Today is a rest from the flood of thoughts and emotions. What is the poem saying to you? Be brief.

---

---

---

_____

_____

_____

_____

_____

_____

_____

**Greater Challenge: Tell your testimony (or at least the most meaningful portion) to someone. Brief thoughts or feelings.**

_____

_____

_____

_____

_____

_____

I AM MORE: The Journey

---

---

---

---

---

---

---

---

---

---

---

---

---

---

---

---

## WEEK THREE

Well, depending on the cycle that was chosen (4 week or 8 week); you are either a quarter of the way or half way through the process. How do you feel? I hope at this point you can proudly say "I AM ME!" I trust you can identify a moment (event) that hindered you from feeling strong, worthy, esteemed, hopeful, powerful, and like so much more.

In the week to come, you will look briefly at your mind, body, spirit, and heart. You will assess those in your circle. Continue to take a look at your "I AM ME!" statement. I do not have the answers for you. I will not attempt to answer the questions of your life. My goal is the same as it was in the prior weeks – To provide a process that helps to organize your thoughts so you may embrace you and the *more* in you". I could supply you with quotes that I love and verses that helped me. But, I won't. Words that strengthened me may have little to no affect on you. You are not alone in this process. By finding your own quotes (as you will be asked to do), it will be more meaningful to you. You will have established a connection to the quote since you were the one who found and read it, and decided that these are the words you need for your life.

From what I have experienced and seen, we have the tendency to identify who we are by those around us. It is true birds of a feather flock together. But, look at yourself. Are your feathers really the same as those flying with you? There is a chance that someone told you that you look like the flock you are flying with but you really don't. Fly with the birds that you believe most resemble you or what you would like to become. Visiting the other birds may be permitted but it's not always advisable. Assess the flock!

This week is meant for you to begin to rebuild and rejuvenate. Through the "I AM ME!" process and the pain assessment, you had to tear yourself apart a little. Well, hopefully, a lot.

We will begin the week by looking at time. I challenge the phrase "time heals all wounds". Time doesn't heal anything. Time is just a measure of how long it takes to heal. It takes time. But, time is not all it takes. God heals all wounds. Be part of your own healing process.

Let's think of ways to build you up. You need to continue to assess. But, you will be assessing your NOW. You know who you are, what makes up who you are, and the pain that prohibited who you could have become. You also know that all those things are merely ingredients in the cake called YOU.

It is time to put the icing on the cake and dress it up. Then the cake will be placed on a platform and presented to the world. But, not quite yet. Let's first work on the parts of you that people can see or sense.

**You are about to become a handsomely decorated cake.**

## WEEK THREE

### DAY ONE

**Thought:** When we go through difficult times, we tend to do what therapists and doctors call self-medicate. We can do this through substance abuse, sexual promiscuity, anger, or any other outlet that will temporarily bring relief or distraction from the pain/memories. Instead of wasting time self-medicating and avoiding the evitable emotional crash, redeem the time.

**Focus:** Time, Healing, Spirituality, Self-Help

**Challenge:** What did you do to self-medicate after the event(s) occurred that you pondered last week? The challenge is to list as much of what you have done as you can. Include positive and negative self-medicating techniques. Expound as much as possible.

e.g.: Thrusting myself into my education (positive)

Over-eating (negative)

_____

_____

_____

_____

_____

_____

_____

_____

**Greater Challenge: Identify a dream or talent that went ignored during or after the event. Can it be resurrected? How?**

_____

_____

I AM MORE: The Journey

_____

_____

_____

_____

_____

_____

_____

_____

_____

_____

_____

_____

## WEEK THREE

## DAY TWO

**Thought:**  Clarity is very important.  Replacing negative thoughts with positive ones is a good way of clearing our minds.  When that becomes too draining, quotes, speeches, and plays can be potential sources of positive material.

**Focus:**  Positivity, Clarity, Power, Strength

**Challenge:**  Look for, write down, and memorize quotes (words heard or read) that have or will inspire you to move forward.  It may be something from this book or a Bible verse.  But, it is important that you find your own source of strength.  Find at least three.

_____

_____

_____

_____

_____

_____

_____

_____

**Greater Challenge:** Write your own "quote". Words that come from your heart and mind that will be your strength in the future. They could help someone else – "Image In" that!

_____

_____

_____

_____

_____

## WEEK THREE

## DAY THREE

**Thought:** Circle. Flock. Posse. Sect. Group. Partner. These are some of the terms used to classify the people with whom we associate. In assessing myself, I found it necessary to assess those around me. I warn you to be prepared for possible aloneness after "trimming the fat" from your circle.

**Focus:** Friendship

**Challenge:** Identify those around you and their roles. Are they protectors or abusers? Do they fortify or weaken you? Assist or prohibit you? Trim the fat.

_____

_____

_____

_____

_____

_____

_____

_____

_____

_____

**Greater Challenge:  Reassess your relationships and eliminate those that are dead weight or detrimental to your                    mental                    health.**

_____

_____

_____

_____

_____

_____

TONISHA "DR. TONI" PINCKNEY

_____

_____

_____

_____

_____

_____

_____

_____

_____

_____

_____

_____

## WEEK THREE

## DAY FOUR

**Thought:** "I heart you." Our society has figured out a way to take the responsibility and power out of one (if not the) most important phrases to us as humans. Love is both a feeling and an action.

**Focus:** Love, Self-worth, Self-esteem

**Challenge:** List people you can say you love. Then tell why you love them. Do you love the same things about yourself? Do you love more things about them than you do yourself?

_____

_____

_____

_____

_____

TONISHA "DR. TONI" PINCKNEY

**Greater Challenge:** List the things you love about yourself. List the things you don't like and why.

Page | 145

I AM MORE: The Journey

_____

_____

_____

_____

_____

_____

_____

_____

_____

_____

_____

_____

_____

_____

_____

## WEEK THREE

## DAY FIVE

**Thought:** Desire plays a very important role in our lives. Most desires are natural. However, when our lives and decisions revolve around inappropriate or misdirected desires such as sex, money, power, drugs, fame, notoriety, etc., it could lead to having improper/unhealthy alliances and relationships. If we don't put them in proper perspective, desires can cause us to lose focus on the other very important aspects of our lives.

**Focus:** Desire, Relationships, Self-Image, Self-Worth

**Challenge:** Identify and write down your strongest active desire that is hindering or distracting you from your goal of becoming *more*. See the list above for examples. ~~Write.~~ Commit to abstain from that desire for the remainder of the process. If you need help, get it. (Husbands and Wives I don't suggest you abstain from sex unless it is with someone outside your union.)

_____

_____

_____

_____

_____

_____

_____

_____

_____

**Greater Challenge:** **Make a list of your sexual relationships. How did those relationships add or take away from your life?**

TONISHA "DR. TONI" PINCKNEY

## WEEK THREE

## DAY SIX

**Thought:** Health is very important to feeling like *more*. You are more confident, decisive, stronger, and in tune with your environment, when you are healthy. Wholeness includes mind, soul, spirit, and BODY.

**Focus:** Health, Wellness, Healing, Strength, Focus

**Challenge:** Assess your eating and exercise habits. What could/should you change? How do you really feel? What hurts? Are there any pains you ignore or are just "used to"? If so, make a doctor/dentist appointment.

_____

_____

_____

_____

_____

_____

_____

_____

_____

_____

_____

**Greater Challenge:** **Find out your family health history. Even if you think you know everything, check again to make sure. Is there mental illness in the family? Get information on how you can protect, prevent, or delay the presentation of these illnesses in your life.**

_____

_____

_____

_____

_____

I AM MORE: The Journey

_____

_____

_____

_____

_____

_____

_____

_____

_____

_____

_____

_____

_____

_____

## WEEK THREE

## DAY SEVEN

**Thought:** Take a deep breath. Inhale. Exhale. RELAX. Relaxation gives time for our minds and bodies to heal. We can find focus and clarity. We can commune with God. Some feel relaxing is just as (if not more) beneficial as sleep.

**Focus:** Relaxation, Rejuvenation, Regeneration, Strength

**Challenge:** Go to the park – Soak in a bath – Get a mani-pedicure – Get a spa treatment – Light some candles and read a book or listen to soft music. Do something that relaxes you and wait to hear your own (and maybe God's) voice. Write down whatever comes to mind.

_____

_____

_____

_____

_____

_____

_____

_____

**Greater Challenge:  Do something to help a person that is having (or recently had) a difficult time to relax; or invite them to relax with you.  Write down the favorite parts of your                                          conversation.**

_____

_____

_____

_____

_____

_____

_____

_____

_____

_____

_____

_____

_____

_____

_____

_____

_____

_____

_____

_____

## WEEK FOUR

Whether you are in the four or eight week cycle – I congratulate you on making it this far. You have proven to yourself that you are committed to your total success. You are dealing with you. You are healing.

By the end of week three, you should have found yourself relaxing. I spent a few days on week three, day seven. After finding out who I am, loving me, assessing my relationships, getting my body right, and *more*, I had to spend a few days relaxing. It's important not to relax too long. Your work is not done. It's time to embrace your destiny. The past is behind you, the winds of emotion are at your back, and your face is looking up. You are ALIVE. You have SURVIVED. You have proven "them" wrong. You have broken out of the shackles of emotional despair. You can walk liberated into your future and be *more*.

Remember: The best part about always seeing

yourself as *more* is that there is no "the end" in your view. Dreams become visions, that turn into realities, which births new dreams, that become new visions, then new realities that... However, once you stop believing there is *more* to you, the cycle ends. You are more than the best you can ever hope to become.

It is by continually assessing yourself, updating your "I AM ME!" statement, and finding the purpose of past issues not dealt with previously that you will always move forward as more.

Destiny, fate, God – do not interfere with your will. I must add that life is a lot easier when you decide that God's will is also your will. Life is smoother and more prosperous when you align your vision with God's vision for your life. He is more, so you are more.

You can be more without God. But, with God the *more* is limitless. Connecting to the source of your empowerment enables you to run even when your mental, physical, and emotional battery is drained. The source will continually sustain you.

Over the next week, you will write your "I AM MORE" statement. This statement, just like your "I AM ME", should change over time. With each passing day, you will realize you are *more*. As you mature and experience life, you will add to your "I AM MORE" statement. Being more brings responsibility. It is not a selfish or self-centered endeavor. You become *more* so that you can help others experience *more*. You are responsible for encouraging your children (or the children around you), ~~your~~ community, ~~your~~ religious assembly, ~~your~~ country, and territory to be *more*. I AM MORE is a collective idea not just an individual one. Each person in the community needs to rise to being *more* so that the community as a whole can collectively rise in pride shouting "I AM MORE!"

The great part is the statement does not die when your spirit leaves this world. Because you are *more*, you will have passed along the desire to be *more* for generations to come. Define what *more* is to you. Commit to being *more*.

**You are just days away from saying "I AM MORE" and meaning it!**

## WEEK FOUR

## DAY ONE

**Thought:** Before you can be *more* you must know who you are. That is the reason for the "I AM ME!" statement. It serves as a record of your strength to endure during difficult times. You know what it took to be you, what it takes to stay you, and what it will take to change you. You are strong!

**Focus:** More Strength

**Challenge:** Write what has, up until this point, made you want to say "I AM MORE!" What have you found out about yourself that proves that you are *more*?

E.g. I was told I am nothing – I AM MORE!

I am not yet sure how to love – I AM MORE!

_____

_____

_____

TONISHA "DR. TONI" PINCKNEY

_____

_____

_____

_____

_____

_____

_____

**Greater Challenge:** **What has changed about and/or around you since the first 4-week cycle? How have you become** **more?**

_____

_____

_____

_____

_____

_____

I AM MORE: The Journey

_____

_____

_____

_____

_____

_____

_____

_____

_____

_____

_____

_____

_____

_____

## WEEK FOUR

## DAY TWO

**Thought:** There can be disappointment in realizing that you are *more*. You discover that people and things try to prevent you from being *more*. There are changes you must make. Since *more* is a fluid concept, you can congratulate yourself on being *more* and identifying those hindrances.

**Focus:** More Determination

**Challenge:** What is going on right now that is preventing you from being *more*? What can you tolerate, adapt, change or totally eliminate?

_____

_____

_____

_____

I AM MORE: The Journey

_____

_____

_____

_____

_____

_____

_____

_____

_____

_____

_____

_____

_____

_____

TONISHA "DR. TONI" PINCKNEY

**Greater Challenge: How has saying "I AM MORE" affected/effected the lives of others in your home, at work, and/or in the community?**

_____

_____

_____

_____

_____

_____

_____

_____

_____

_____

_____

_____

## WEEK FOUR

## DAY THREE

**Thought:** The label on food, clothing, or virtually any product plays a powerful role in the decision whether or not to buy it. Although placement is important, the label tells how the makers, critics, and testers feel about the product. By looking at the label you feel what they feel. Tobacco=dangerous Vitamins=Healthy

**Focus:** More Positivity, More Self-Esteem

**Challenge:** List the negative and positive labels that have been placed on you. Then write I AM MORE after each.

e.g. Ms. Jane is indecisive – I AM MORE

Mr. Paul has a six-pack – I AM MORE

_____

_____

_____

_____

_____

_____

_____

_____

_____

**Greater Challenge:  List the positive and negative labels that have been placed on your community. Then write "I AM            MORE"            after            each.**

_____

_____

_____

_____

I AM MORE: The Journey

**WEEK FOUR**

**DAY FOUR**

**Thought:** There is so much to God. The Bible says we were created in the image of God. Whenever we try to list the attributes of God, we can always come up with one more. So we can say God is just *more*. If He is more, then you, me, and we are all *more*. He bridged the gap between our past and ~~our~~ future through Jesus' resurrection.

**Focus:** More Belief, More Spirituality, More Inspiration

**Challenge:** Write attributes of God ~~as~~ that you know or have been told. After each write "He is more, so I am more". Refer to the poem for an example. This section can also be used to be thankful for blessings He has provided.

_____

_____

_____

_____

_____

_____

_____

_____

**Greater Challenge:** Write miracles, unexplainable events, or changes for the better in your life which brought about by Divine protection. After each write "He is more, so I am more".

_____

_____

_____

_____

_____

TONISHA "DR. TONI" PINCKNEY

_____

_____

_____

_____

_____

_____

_____

_____

_____

_____

_____

_____

_____

_____

_____

_____

## WEEK FOUR

## DAY FIVE

**Thought:** Assess your power. The true test of our level of self-worth, self-esteem, self-love, etc., is when someone asks us to tell them a little about ourselves. Some call it an elevator speech or a 30-sec bio. No matter how you describe it, what you say sends signals to the listener about how they should feel about you.

**Focus:** More Respect, More Esteem, More Confidence

**Challenge:** Write a quick "I AM MORE" speech that you could read to a prospective employer, client, partner, school WITHOUT saying I AM MORE. (Hint: Look at your "I AM MORE statements so far)

_____

_____

TONISHA "DR. TONI" PINCKNEY

_____

_____

_____

_____

_____

_____

_____

_____

**Greater Challenge: What was the main driving force that helped you along in the process? How can you help others come to the realization that they are _more_? e.g. Buy them their own copy of this book.**

_____

_____

_____

_____

I AM MORE: The Journey

_____

_____

_____

_____

_____

_____

_____

_____

_____

_____

_____

_____

_____

_____

## WEEK FOUR

## DAY SIX

**Thought:** Words are very powerful. They can wound or heal. I use my poetry to help myself and others heal. Like a lot of children, I heard horrible statements that wounded me for life (or so I thought). Take on the responsibility of not speaking or allowing negative words to be spoken to children. Encourage them and understand the important role you play in their lives (no matter how brief).

**Focus:** More Responsibility, More Nurturing, More Positive

**Challenge:** List negative statements made to you when you were a child (or even now). After each write "I AM MORE".

---

---

---

_____

_____

_____

_____

_____

_____

_____

_____

**Greater Challenge:  Read "I AM A CHILD, BUT I AM MORE"**

**to     a     child.     What     was     their     reaction?**

_____

_____

_____

_____

_____

_____

TONISHA "DR. TONI" PINCKNEY

_____

_____

_____

_____

_____

_____

_____

_____

_____

_____

_____

_____

_____

_____

## WEEK FOUR

## DAY SEVEN

**Thought:** Today is _____ (write date). This is day one of you living the life of *more*. Walk in excellence and trust God for perfection. Know that you are *more*. Nothing and no one can change that – not even you. If this is your first time through the cycle – complete it again soon. Congratulations!

**Focus:** ENJOY *more*, LOVE *more*, HOPE *more*, BELIEVE *more*, RESPECT *more*, REFLECT *more*, CRY *more*, LAUGH *more* -- *more! more! more!*

**Challenge:** Write a covenant with yourself to see and believe that you are *more*. Promise to see others as *more*. Vow to connect to a power source that is *more*. Write what you feel, believe, or want to believe. Then go relax!

_____

_____

_____

_____

_____

_____

_____

_____

_____

**Greater Challenge:** Write a promise to help a child, community, spouse, etc., become _more_. Whether or not you show them the promise – keep it!

_____

_____

_____

_____

I AM MORE: The Journey

_____

_____

_____

_____

_____

_____

_____

_____

_____

_____

_____

_____

_____

_____

## NOTES:

_____

_____

_____

_____

_____

_____

_____

_____

_____

_____

_____

_____

_____

_____

NOTES:

_____

_____

_____

_____

_____

_____

_____

_____

_____

_____

_____

_____

NOTES:

_____

_____

_____

_____

_____

_____

_____

_____

_____

_____

_____

NOTES:

I AM MORE: The Journey

_____

_____

_____

_____

_____

_____

_____

_____

_____

_____

_____

_____

_____

## To Book Dr. Toni as a Speaker or Lecturer:

Motivating and inspiring others is a deep passion for Dr. Toni.

She is available to speak to your business, organization, support group, school, university, or church. If you would like to book her you may contact I AM MORE, LLC via email at:

bookings@iammoreonline.com.

## OTHER CONTACT INFORMATION:

To get further information: info@iammoreonline.com.

Visit the website: www.iammoreonline.com

Like her on Facebook: www.facebook.com/IAMMORE

Follow on twitter: @IAMMORE

Instagram: @iammorepics

# THE AUTHOR

Dr. Tonisha M. Pinckney, a native of Newark, NJ, is dedicated to educating and advocating for others. With a wide range of expertise, supported by 16 years of combined experience, Dr. Pinckney developed a series of individual and community tools. Dr. Pinckney is a Criminal Justice and Criminology expert, Forensic Criminologist, and Forensic Accountant, is an Assistant Professor of Criminal Justice and Legal Studies at Newbury College and is listed as an adjunct faculty member at the University of Massachusetts - Lowell. Dr. Pinckney is an outspoken author, advocate, and lecturer on issues of racial, socioeconomic, and gender disparities. Dr. Pinckney has a special passion for helping adult and child victims and offenders of sexual assault and domestic violence. Fueled by her own experiences, she authored two books discussing domestic violence, sexual assault, depression and suicide, and parenting – I AM MORE – The Journey (2009) and I AM MORE: Surviving Survival (2013). Dr. Pinckney is the founder of a new not-for-profit organization, I AM MORE Institute for Excellence and Social Responsibility. Recognizing the importance of saying, "I AM

MORE!" Dr. Pinckney registered it as a trademark.

Combining her passions for social change, her dissertation, Children present on the scene upon police arrival at an intimate partner violence incident: Race, police action, and officer-initiated social support, examined whether the needs of children exposed to IPV and the race of a couple factor into an officer's decisions as to whether to take law enforcement action (arrest or issue a citation) and initiate social support for the exposed child and victim-partner.

"I AM MORE – the Journey" was born from the adversities Dr. Toni faced throughout her life. In order for her to survive life's hardships and pains, she had to learn that she was not limited to being a product of her past. In fact, she was more. She was a facilitator of her future. Dr. Toni uses her life lessons to inspire men, women, and children to become 'powerfully productive" not "allow[ing] their reasons to fail to become their excuses for failure – excellence NOT excuse!". Dr. Toni, a survivor of multiple rapes, years of domestic violence, and emotional abuse says, "I want to inspire inner strength and introduce spiritual empowerment in the lives of those with broken hearts and spirits".

I AM MORE: The Journey

"There is nothing stopping you from becoming "more" except the thought that you are "less". You are "more". So allow the words to echo in your mind, heart, and spirit!"

Yes, I AM MORE!

www.ingramcontent.com/pod-product-compliance
Lightning Source LLC
Chambersburg PA
CBHW031512040426
42445CB00009B/185